Contents

Communities

People live in communities. They live near each other and help each other.

People work together in a community.

Dentists in the community

Dentists work in communities.

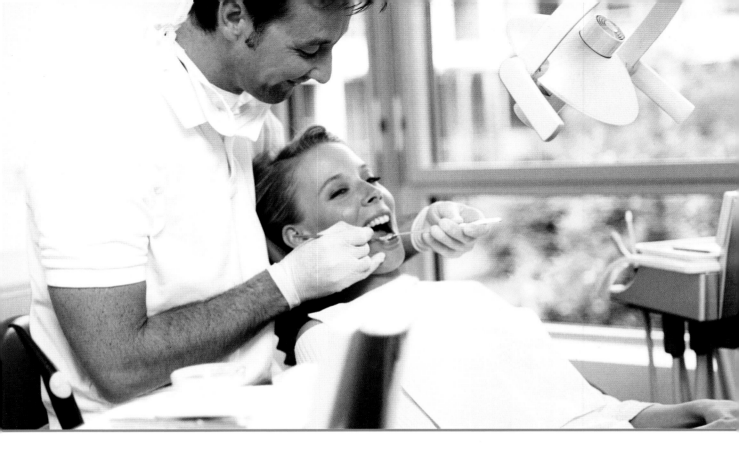

Dentists look after people's teeth.

What dentists do

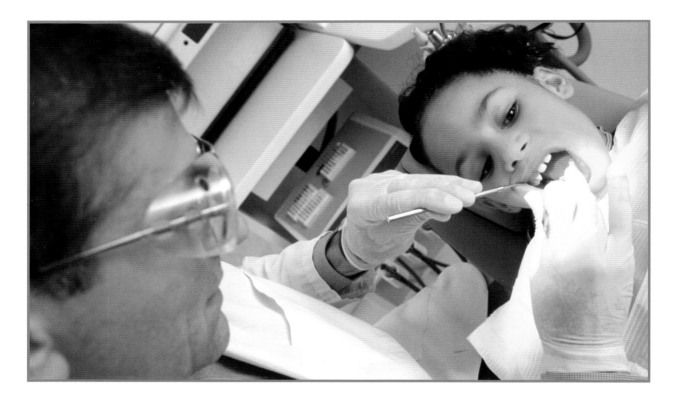

Dentists check teeth to make sure they are not going bad.

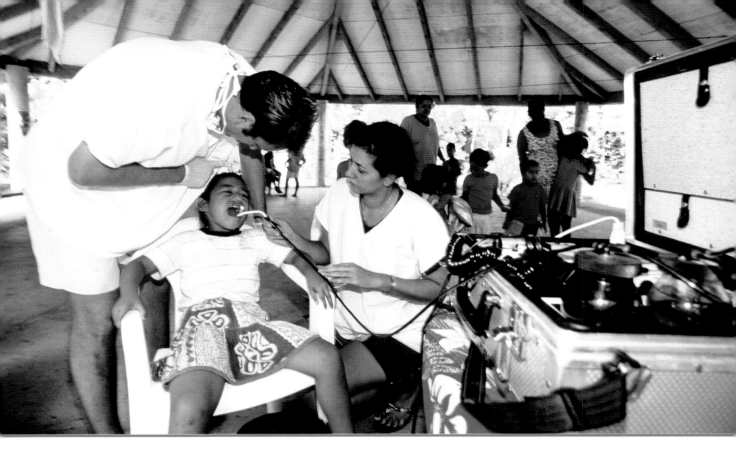

Dentists clean people's teeth with a special tool.

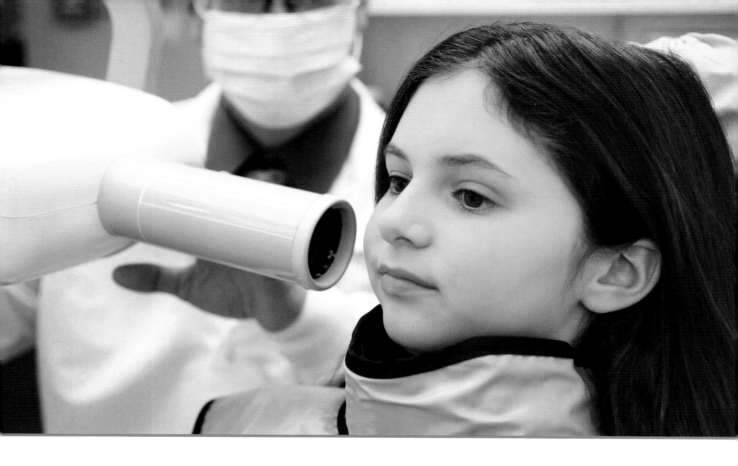

Dentists take X-rays of teeth to make sure they are not going bad.

This X-ray is a picture of the girl's teeth.

What dentists use

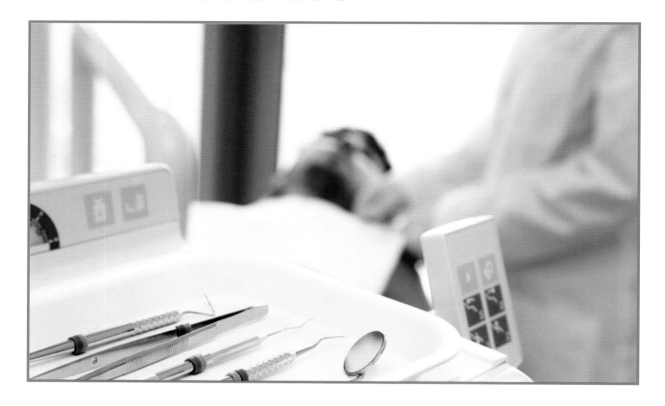

Dentists use lots of different tools.

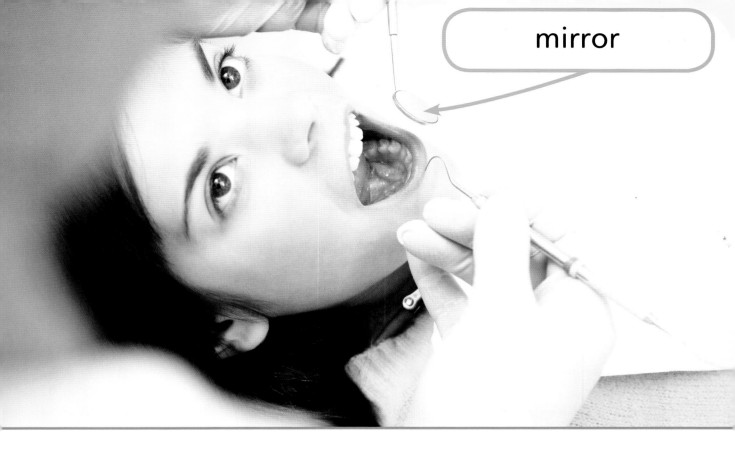

mirror

Dentists use mirrors to look at teeth.

Where dentists work

Dentists work in offices.

Dentists work in clinics.

People who work with dentists

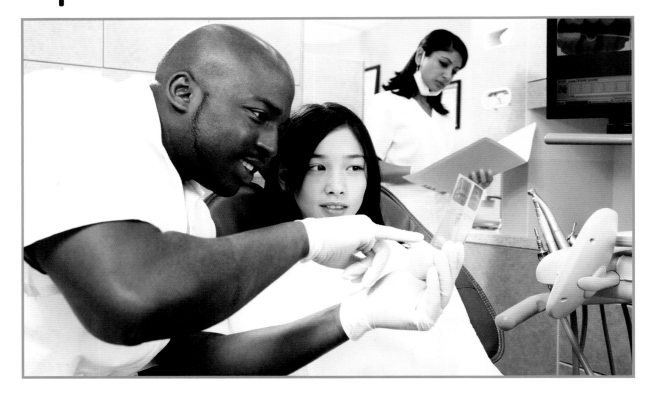

Dentists work with other people.

This person greets people.

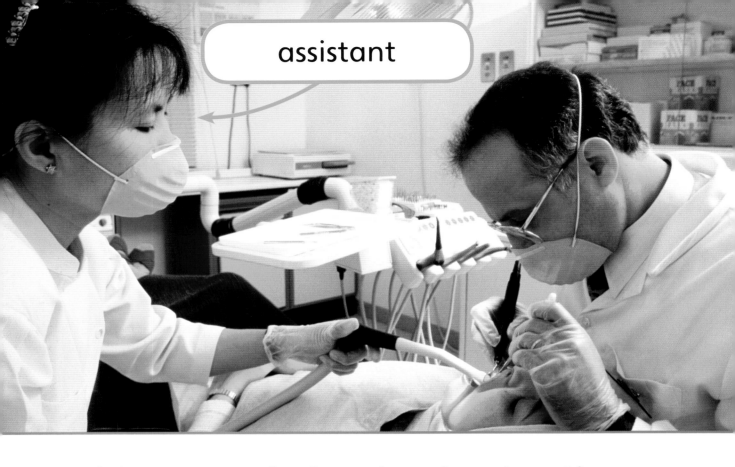

assistant

This person helps the dentist. She gives the dentist the right tools.

hygienist

This person helps to clean teeth so they do not go bad.

How dentists help us

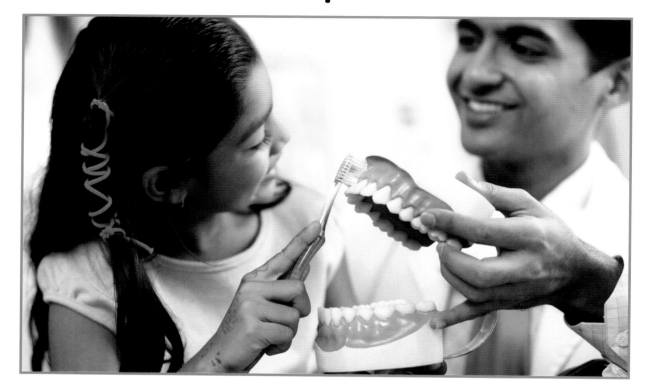

Dentists help keep our teeth healthy.
They show us how to brush our teeth.

Dentists help the community.

Picture glossary

 **community** group of people living and working in the same area

 **office** place where a dentist works

 **X-ray** photo of the inside of a person's body

Index

Notes for parents and teachers

This series introduces readers to the lives of different community workers, and explains some of the different jobs they perform around the world. Some of the locations featured include Hanover, Germany (page 4); Ua Pou, French Polynesia (page 9); Chicago, USA (page 14), and Siem Reap, Cambodia (page 15).

Before reading
Talk to the children about the work of a dentist. Ask if they have been to the dentist. Have they ever had toothache? What did it feel like? Why do they think people get toothache? What different people did they see at the dentist's?

After reading
• Help the children to draw large smiley faces with teeth. Put these on the wall as a collage.
• To the tune of "Here we go round the mulberry bush" sing the following and encourage the children to make the actions:
This is the way we brush our teeth...
This is the way we rinse our mouth...
This is the way we smile at our friends...